THE RICHEST JEWELS

THE
RICHEST
JEWELS

edited by
Kenneth D. Macleod

FREE PRESBYTERIAN PUBLICATIONS

FREE PRESBYTERIAN PUBLICATIONS
133 Woodlands Road
Glasgow
G3 6LE

Most of the pieces in this book were previously published in
The Young People's Magazine

This collection first published 1993

ISBN 0 902506 33 1

Origination by
Settle Graphics
Settle, North Yorkshire

Printed by
The Craven Herald & Pioneer
Skipton, North Yorkshire

Contents

"That Is Mine"

I WANT to tell you about a wealthy and proud landowner who lived in England long ago. A godly farmer called on him one day to ask a favour. Before the farmer was able to ask for the favour, the landowner said he wished to show him round his estate. The farmer agreed.

They walked together for quite a long way until they reached the top of a hill. From there they could see the estate all around. It was a very large estate, which the landowner probably inherited when his father died.

The landowner proudly pointed out his fields. "These are mine," he said to the farmer. He pointed out his woods, and said, "These are mine". "And these are mine also," he said, pointing out farm buildings and houses. Finally he said to the farmer, "Indeed, everything you can see is mine".

The godly farmer was thoughtful for a while. Then, pointing up to heaven, he looked at the landowner and asked, "Does that belong to you as well?", meaning, was there a place for him in heaven.

The landowner could not say a word because the farmer's question went to his heart like an arrow. He knew that while he had lands in this world, he had no place in heaven. He was proud of everything that was his but he did not have the one thing needful. He was busy making money from his estate, but he was not laying up treasure in heaven.

The good farmer's question was blessed to the landowner, and he began to think about these words of Jesus: "But seek ye first the kingdom of God and His righteousness; and all these things shall be added unto you."

The day came when the landowner found the Lord and His salvation. So now he had an inheritance in heaven. If you are born again and believe in Jesus the Bible says that you have "an inheritance incorruptible, and undefiled, and that fadeth not away, reserved in heaven for you".

I don't know if the farmer got his favour from the landowner, but I do know that the landowner got a great

favour from the farmer when he asked him that solemn question, ''Does that belong to you as well?''.

The landowner was given a greater favour when God gave him a right to the inheritance in heaven. He now had this treasure in heaven and he was able to say, ''That, by God's grace, is mine''. May it be yours also. Seek it with your whole heart.

N. M. Ross

The Richest Jewels

IN the Bible we read about jewels. There were the jewels in the breastplate of the high priest in Israel. We also read about jewels of silver, gold and pearls which women wore. In the New Testament we are told about a very costly pearl which a merchant wanted so much that he sold all his belongings to get money to buy it.

The Bible itself is a jewel. David the Psalmist said that it was more precious to him than lots of gold.

Long ago there was a godly nurse who had to look after a lady who was ill. One day the lady said to her nurse, ''Bring me my jewels''.

When the nurse brought them the lady said, "Now, Nurse, wouldn't you like to have some of these jewels?".

The nurse replied, "No madam, for I have jewels which are much more precious than these".

"How can that be?" asked the lady in surprise. "Let me see one!"

"My jewels are in this book," said the nurse, picking up her Bible. "Let me show you some of them." She then read to the lady some of the precious verses in this precious book.

For some days the nurse showed her sick patient more and more of the jewels of the Bible, including the "great and precious promises" of the gospel. God blessed His Word to the sick woman, and the Bible became precious to her — more precious than her jewels. Is the Bible precious to you?

Now, I'm sure you have heard that you must search in the Bible for "the Pearl of great price". Do you know who He is?

I will try to explain by telling you another story which is quite like the one I have just told you. Here it is.

A very rich lady came from Java to live in England long ago. She had many valuable jewels which she loved.

One day she said to her maid, who came from Scotland, "I think England is a poor place".

"Why so, madam?" asked the maid.

"When I look out on the streets I don't see ladies with jewels on. In my country the ladies wear diamonds and pearls and other jewels. We dig into our hills and get gold and silver and precious stones. You dig into your hills and get nothing like them."

"Yes, madam," said the maid, "but we have a pearl in this country which is called 'the Pearl of great price'."

"Have you indeed?" said the lady. "I would like to get it."

"O!" said the nurse, "this Pearl is not to wear, and you cannot buy it with money. They who have it cannot lose it. They are at peace, and have all they wish for."

"Indeed!" said the lady. "What can this pearl be?"

"This Pearl," said the maid, "is the Lord Jesus Christ who came into the world to save sinners." The maid then told her mistress that everyone is a sinner and that any sinner who believes in Christ is saved from his sins. "So precious is Christ to those who believe in Him," she said, "that they count all things but loss for the excellency of the knowledge of Him."

The lady was led by God to seek a better treasure than her jewels, and she found "the Pearl of great price", Jesus Christ. So precious did He become to her that soon after, when she was dying, she ordered that her jewels be sold and that the money be used to send the goods news about "the Pearl of great price" to those who have not heard it.

Are *you* seeking for "the Pearl of great price"? He says, "Seek, and ye shall find".

N. M. Ross

God Is Our Refuge
and Strength

GOD is our refuge and our strength,
In straits a present aid;
Therefore, although the earth remove,
We will not be afraid:

Though hills amidst the seas be cast;
Though waters roaring make,
And troubled be; yea, though the hills
By swelling seas do shake.

A river is, whose streams do glad
The city of our God;
The holy place, wherein the Lord
Most high hath His abode.

God in the midst of her doth dwell;
Nothing shall her remove:
The Lord to her an helper will,
And that right early, prove.

Psalm 46:1-5

Most Precious
Treasure

DIAMONDS are among the most precious things in the world. One of the royal jewels is the famous Koh-i-noor diamond. It is one of the most precious stones in the whole world. *Koh-i-noor* means *mountain of light,* and this is a very suitable name because dazzling light flashes out from this very large diamond.

Lord Lawrence was a very important man in India. He had to arrange for the diamond to be sent to Queen Victoria in London. As he held it in his hand, his old Indian servant looked at it but did not realise how precious it was. He saw that it was pretty, but he thought that it was worth very little. "It is nothing, sahib," he said, "but a bit of glass."

Do you know what is the most precious thing in the world, more precious than the most precious jewel? If you say, "The Bible!" that is the right answer. David says in a Psalm that the Word of God — he means the Bible — is more precious than the very best gold. And Solomon says that the truth of God's Word is more precious than all gold or silver or precious stones.

It is very sad that many people do not think that the Bible is worth much at all. Just as the Indian servant said that the Koh-i-noor diamond was only a bit of glass, they think that the Bible is only an ordinary book. I hope that the words of God in the Bible will be so precious to you that you will be saying about them:

> They more than gold, yea, much fine gold
> To be desired are.

(Psalm 19:10)

The Bible is the most precious book in the world because it tells us about the precious Saviour, Jesus Christ. Although most people do not think much of Him, the Bible tells us that He is the Pearl of great price. Pray to God that He would make Jesus Christ precious to you. And that He would make the Bible precious to you too.

N. M. Ross

David and Goliath

EVERYBODY in King Saul's army was very frightened. Saul was king of Israel, but their enemies, the Philistines, had come to fight them. What was so very frightening was that their giant, Goliath, came twice every day to shout to Saul and his men. Yes, Goliath was very, very big and powerful. He was covered with lots of heavy armour, and he carried a huge spear. Every day he asked Saul and the Israelites to send just one man to fight against him. If Goliath won, then all the Israelites would have to become slaves to the Philistines. But if Goliath was killed, the Philistines would become slaves to the Israelites.

Day after day Goliath came to shout his challenge to Saul and his men. But what could they do? Nobody felt strong enough or brave enough to go to fight against such a big and powerful man. Surely no one could possibly kill him, they thought. They did not know what to do.

Did anyone think of asking God to help them? Surely there were some men in that army who knew that only God could help them — some men who really knew God and often prayed to Him. But, sadly, Saul was not one of them; he was not a friend of God.

Among the soldiers in the army there were three young men from Bethlehem. One day their father Jesse decided to send them some food. So he called David his youngest son to take the food to his brothers and to find out how they were getting on. David got up early in the morning and went to where the army had camped.

While David was talking to his brothers he heard Goliath once more shouting to the Israelites and asking them to send someone to fight against him. Goliath had come every day for forty days now, but still nobody felt strong enough to go to fight him. But David did not feel like that. He started telling people that he would go to fight against Goliath. His brothers thought that it was very stupid of him even to think of it. At last someone took David to the king. But would it be wise for the king to allow David to fight Goliath? Wasn't Goliath far too strong for David?

Saul looked at David, but he was sure that David was far too young. And he had never before fought a battle. But David told the king about how he had looked after his father's sheep. He spoke about the day when a lion came and took away a lamb. David saved the lamb and, when the lion turned on himself, he killed it. And when a bear took away one of the lambs he killed it too.

David knew that he could do the same with the Philistines' hero. Why? Because God would help him, just as He had helped him against the lion and the bear. He knew that Goliath was not just speaking against Israel, but also against Israel's God, who is the true God. So David told Saul that God, who had delivered him from the lion and the bear would deliver from the Philistines too.

Saul decided that David should go to fight Goliath; after all, no one else was prepared to try. He gave David his own armour and a helmet for his head. David tried them on and he took the sword that Saul had given him. But he was not comfortable; he had never tried on clumsy armour before. He knew that he would get on much better without it, so he took it off and gave everything back to Saul.

David went away with only a stick in his hand, the stick that he used when he was looking after his father's sheep. But, when he reached a little river, he stopped to choose five smooth stones. He picked them up and put them in the shepherd's bag which he was carrying. There was one other thing that David had with him; probably he took it out of his bag then. It was his sling; it would be far more useful to him than the best sword that Saul could give him.

When Goliath saw David, he thought it was so silly — after forty days the Israelites could only send this young fellow, and he had nothing more than a stick to fight with! So he shouted bad things at David; he was quite sure he could easily kill David, and he said so.

David was just as sure that he could kill Goliath. But did Goliath not have a big sword and spear and someone to walk in front of him with a big shield? Yes, David knew it, and he told Goliath that he knew it. But David had something better and stronger, and he spoke about that to Goliath too. He had God with him, and he was looking to God to help him.

As Goliath came closer, David put his hand into his bag and took out one of the stones which he had picked up at the river. He put the stone into the sling and, as soon as David was ready, he sent the stone flying through the air — to where the Philistine giant was standing. David's first stone hit Goliath's forehead, and at once he fell down on the ground. Goliath was dead.

Of course, the Philistines did not expect this and at once they all ran away, with the Israelites all chasing after them. Whoever had forgotten God, David had not — and God did not forget David.

Do you remember God when you know that something is wrong? I hope so. But I would be happier if I thought that you remembered that there is always something wrong — because you are a sinner. Always ask God to help you — and especially to forgive your sins for Jesus' sake.

K. D. Macleod

Wise Creatures

OUR dog seems so wise sometimes. She somehow knows when I am about to go for a walk, even when I say nothing. She becomes very alert. As I put my jacket on in the hall she bounces about and barks excitedly. She knows she is going for a walk!

There are other creatures who are very wise. The Bible tells us about four creatures which are very small but which are "exceeding wise" — that is, very, very wise. You may read about them in the Book of Proverbs, chapter 30, verses 24 to 28. Why not look for these verses now, and read them?

First, there are the *ants*. "The ants are a people not strong, yet they prepare their meat in the summer" (verse 25). How wise these tiny insects are! Although they are weak, they work very hard in summer gathering food and storing it in their nest in readiness for

winter. When winter comes, they are prepared.

Should you not be wise like the ants? Yes, indeed! You should be getting ready in the summer-time of your young days for the end of your life, the awful winter of death. Are you prepared for that winter; prepared to die; and so prepared to meet God and to enter heaven? Remember the Bible says, "Prepare to meet thy God". Jesus says, "Be ye therefore also ready". Do not leave it till it is too late.

The next wise creature is the *coney*. Conies are rather like guinea-pigs, and they live among the rocks in some eastern countries. "The conies are but a feeble folk, yet make they their houses in the rocks" (verse 26). They are lively little animals but they are not able to defend themselves against bigger and stronger creatures.

How can they be safe? By running into their little homes in the crevices of the rocks and hiding there.

You too are in danger. If you are not saved you are in danger of being punished for your sins. How can you escape that punishment and be safe? Only by running to Jesus Christ, the Saviour of sinners, who is called, "The Rock of Salvation". Everyone who has been made willing and able to believe in Him has hurried to this Rock, and is hiding in this Rock. I hope that you too will hurry to this safe place.

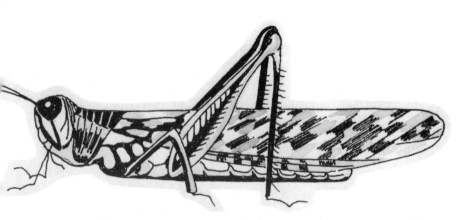

Another wise creature is the *locust.* Locusts look like our grasshoppers, but bigger, and they often fly together and feed together in great swarms or "bands". "The locusts have no king, yet go they forth all of them by bands" (verse 27). Although they do not have a leader, and although they are so many, they keep together in groups and work together in an orderly way.

We need to be wise like them, in our families, so that we would keep together, work together and be kind to one another. Quarrelling, fighting and falling out with one another are all very bad. And how important it is to be part of the family of God's children. I hope that you will be really one of God's children, loving to be with them, and keeping close to them as they travel to heaven together.

The last little wise creature is the *spider.* Verse 28 tells us, "The spider taketh hold with her hands, and is in kings' palaces". She makes her web not only in houses but also in palaces. See how she keeps on working and does not give up. She keeps on working until every thread of her web is finished. If her web is broken she repairs it. If it is swept away she begins again.

Do you remember the story about Robert Bruce, a king of Scotland, who was once very sad because he had failed, time after time, to get his kingdom back from the English king? One day, in his sadness, he saw a spider trying to reach a certain part of the ceiling. Time after time it tried, but each time it failed. At last it seemed to have given up altogether. But no! it tried again; and this time it succeeded. Bruce was so encouraged by what he saw that he thought, ''I, too, will try again''. He tried again, defeated the English at Bannockburn in 1314, and won his kingdom.

You too must be like the spider. You must keep on trying: trying to do what is right even although you will be failing often. Especially, you must keep on seeking the Lord and not give up because you do not find Him as soon as you thought you would. You should seek Him all the harder and with your whole heart, for He is saying to you, ''Ye shall . . . find me when ye shall search for me with all your heart''.

N. M. Ross

The Victoria Falls

THE Victoria Falls on the Zambesi River in Africa is one of the largest waterfalls in the world and was discovered for the outside world by the explorer and missionary, David Livingstone. On a recent visit to the Falls there was so much spray in the air that we could see very little, and we were soaked in a few minutes!

A few miles away, however, people are both short of water and hungry, because of lack of rain or the means of irrigating the land with water from the river. This is so even although there have been many ideas and plans to make use of the abundant supply of water in the river.

Just as these people long to have a plentiful supply of water and food, so people everywhere thirst and hunger in other ways. We all want happiness, we long to have all our wishes granted and to have all our desires satisfied. And we may be very dissatisfied and unhappy because our plans and longings are not fulfilled.

Yet Jesus Christ has an abundant supply of satisfaction; especially He has a plentiful supply of gospel blessings to give to those who come to Him. That supply which He has for sinners is like a full well of water — like an overflowing spring — like a broad and deep river of pure water. That water which Jesus gives is ''the water of life'' and is much easier to get than the waters of the Zambesi River. Christ has made all preparations

23

and all that is necessary is to come to Him and ask Him for this water of life which will satisfy the longing soul. If we get these gospel blessings of eternal life, pardon of our sins and peace with God, then all other kinds of blessings will also be given to us.

Do you remember the story of the woman of Samaria? Jesus said to her that if she asked Him He would give her "living water". "Whosoever drinketh of the water that I shall give him shall never thirst," Jesus said, "but the water that I shall give him shall be in him a well of water springing up into everlasting life." The woman of Samaria then asked Him, "Sir, give me this water". She did not really understand what that water was; but Jesus explained things to her and gave her that spiritual water of life. In other words, He gave her the great gift of eternal life.

I hope that you will be made willing to go to Him for this water of life. He is saying to us, "If any man thirst, let him come unto me, and drink", and, "Whosoever will, let him take the water of life freely".

M. Graham

The Best Path

THERE is a path that leads to God,
All others go astray;
Narrow and pleasant is the road,
And Christians love the way.

It leads straight through this world of sin,
And dangers must be passed;
But those who boldly walk therein
Will get to heaven at last.

How shall a little pilgrim dare
The dangerous path to tread?
For on the way is many a snare
For youthful travellers spread;

While the broad road, where thousands go,
Lies near, and opens fair;
And many turn aside, I know,
To walk with sinners there.

But lest my feeble steps should slide,
Or wander from Thy way,
Lord, condescend to be my Guide,
And I shall never stray.

A Boy That
Could be Trusted

HANS was a shepherd boy who lived in Germany long ago. One day, as he was carefully watching his sheep grazing at the edge of a forest, a hunter suddenly came riding out of the forest. When he caught sight of the shepherd boy he called, ''My lad, can you tell me the way to the nearest town?''.

''There is only a sheep path leading there from here,'' said Hans. ''But it leads into so many other paths, I am afraid you will never find your way.''

''Would you like to jump up behind me on my horse, and show me the path then?'' asked the hunter.

''O, sir,'' said Hans, ''I cannot do that. I have to look after the sheep in case a wolf attacks them.''

''I'll pay you more than the cost of any sheep that will be lost, if you will show me the way to town,'' said the hunter.

''But I promised to stay with the sheep. My master could not trust me again if I left them,'' said Hans.

''Well, let me stay with them,'' was the laughing reply, ''while you run and find a guide for me.''

''But the sheep would not know your voice,'' said Hans. ''If you called them back from danger they would not come.''

"But I could ride after them. Can't you trust me?"

"No," replied Hans. You try to make me break my promise to my master. How do I know you will keep your word to me."

At that the hunter laughed again. "You are right, my boy," he said. "I wish I could trust my servants as well as your master can trust you. Point out the right direction for me and I will try to find the town myself."

Just then, some hunters rode out of the forest. When they saw the hunter beside Hans, they shouted for joy.

"Our Prince!" they cried. "We thought you were lost."

Not many days after that, a servant came to take Hans to the Prince's castle. "Hans," said the Prince as soon as he arrived, "I want you to leave your sheep and come to serve me. You are a boy whom I am sure I can trust."

This made Hans very happy, but still he did not forget his duty to his own master. "If my master can get another boy to take care of the sheep, I will come," he replied gladly.

So back he went to be a shepherd lad once more. It was not long before another boy was found to take his place, and then he went to the castle to serve the Prince. He became a most faithful and trusted follower of the Prince, because he had learned to obey and to keep his promises.

Can you be trusted to do what you are told when your parents or teachers are away? Can they say to you, "You are someone whom we are sure we can trust"? A person who can be trusted is described as reliable, dependable, trustworthy and faithful, and this is what God wants you to be at all times. Jesus said, "He that is faithful in that which is least is faithful also in much" (Luke 16:10).

If you are honest, dependable and diligent, then you will be trusted by others. The Bible says, "Seest thou a man diligent in his business? He shall stand before kings" (Proverbs 22:29). So it happened to Hans.

Preparations

SCHOOL has started here at Ingwenya in Zimbabwe after our summer holidays (which are in December and January here). But although the new term has already begun, boys and girls still arrive at our door at all hours; some have walked long distances; some have come with relatives we already know. All have one plea: ''Please, may I have a place in your school?''.

Mostly the answer to them is, ''Sorry, it is too late''. They should have applied earlier and sat an entrance test before the term started. Now the school is full. So they have to be sent away because they made no preparations. Sometimes a boy or girl who applied in time but has failed the test will come hoping it was a mistake, or thinking that they can sneak in unnoticed. They also are sent away!

John Bunyan, in his book called *The Pilgrim's Progress,* tells of a pilgrim who reached right to the gates of heaven. He thought he would get into heaven, but he was not allowed because he was not prepared. He did not have a robe and scroll. He found the way into heaven barred, and he was sent by another door down into hell.

You may not have to search for a place in school, but all of us have to prepare for new beginnings. You may have to prepare to move to a new home; and of course you have to prepare to begin a new term in school. You perhaps prepare by getting new clothes, or books, or pens, pencils and rubbers. Sometimes you make a lot of effort to get just what you want in this life.

Here is a question for you: Have you made preparation for the life after this life — I mean, for eternal life in heaven? In school we learn that a line is made up of an infinite number of tiny dots — so many that they can never be counted. It is impossible to imagine how many that is. That is what eternity is like in comparison with our life here. Eternity is infinite or endless, and our life is like one tiny dot in comparison with eternity.

In your short life in this world you have to prepare for eternity. Are you prepared by being born again and by believing in Jesus Christ? Do you have the robe of His righteousness covering your soul? Do you have the scroll which will allow you into heaven, so that you may live happily there for ever? Jesus said to His disciples about heaven, ''I go to prepare a place for you''. Are you prepared for that glorious place which He has prepared for His people?

M. Graham

The Youngest Son
Chosen

LONG ago, King Saul of Israel did many wrong things and God was angry. God said to His prophet Samuel that another king would have to be chosen instead of Saul.

When a new king was chosen in Israel in those days, oil was poured on his head. The pouring of the oil was called *anointing,* and it was a sign that the king was chosen to serve God.

God sent Samuel to anoint the new king. But who was to be the new king? God told Samuel that he was to go to Bethlehem and anoint one of the sons of a man called Jesse, who lived there.

When Samuel arrived at Jesse's home he asked that Jesse's sons would be brought to him. First came Eliab. He was very tall and handsome and really quite kingly. Samuel thought that this son would surely be the one to be anointed. But God said to Samuel that Eliab was not to be anointed.

The other sons, all six of them, came one by one and stood before Samuel; but as each one came God said to Samuel that he was not to be chosen.

Then Samuel asked Jesse if these were all the sons he had. ''There remaineth yet the youngest,'' replied Jesse, ''and, behold, he keepeth the sheep.'' That son was David.

"Send and fetch him," Samuel told Jesse.

When David came, God told Samuel, "Arise, anoint him; for this is he". So the youngest son was chosen to be king, and he began to rule after Saul was killed in battle.

Here are some verses which tell the story of David's young days:

When David was a shepherd boy
He did what he was told,
He watched the flocks round Bethlehem
In rain and shine and cold.

And when a roaring lion came
And then a growling bear,
He asked the Lord to strengthen him
And slew them then and there.

He also slew Goliath bold
With simple stone and sling.
So God chose out the shepherd boy
To be His people's king.

N. M. Ross

An Indian's Hope

IT was hot, very hot, as groups of travellers trudged wearily along the dusty road under the Indian sun. For one old man travelling alone it was too much, and he collapsed at the roadside. There was a godly missionary on the same road. When he saw the Indian collapse he went to his side. It was clear that the poor man was dying. The missionary said gently, "Brother, what is your hope?".

It needed a big effort for the Indian to answer. But he lifted himself up a little and weakly said, "The blood of Jesus Christ cleanseth from all sin".

The missionary was amazed to hear that. He thought that the man was a heathen, like so many others in India, and that he did not know anything about God. "How could he have learned about Jesus?'' the missionary asked himself. And just then he noticed a piece of paper in the man's hand. Although the Indian was now dead his hand still held it.

What was it? The missionary was so surprised and so happy when he looked at it. It was a page from the Bible. On that page was the first chapter of the First Epistle of John. If you look up verse 7 in that chapter you will find the words the man said.

God had taught him that he was a sinner, and that Jesus Christ takes away sin because He has died to save sinners.

Will *you* pray that God would teach this to you too; and that He would really cleanse you from all *your* sin?

K. D. Macleod

What God Teaches

SCHOOL is very important. Some of you, I know, like school very much, but some of you are not fond of it and you are very glad when the bell tells you that it is time to go home.

Why is school important? It is important because it is the place where you learn to read and write and count. Would it not be very difficult for you if you could not read an interesting book or write a letter to a friend? Would it not be difficult if you could not count your pocket money? So you really need to be taught, don't you?

There is another kind of teaching that you need. It is only God who can give you this teaching. He teaches the Bible to His own people in a special way by His Holy Spirit. You must read your Bible and ask God to teach you.

He teaches His people to know that they are sinners who need the only Saviour, Jesus Christ. I hope you will pray the same prayer as a Highland girl of long ago, "Lord, show me myself".

He teaches them to know Himself as the One who forgives sin, and to know His Son as the One who saves from sin. I hope you will also pray, "Lord show me Thyself".

He teaches them how to live day by day. I hope you will pray, "Shew me Thy ways, O Lord; teach me Thy paths".

He is saying, "Come, ye children, hearken unto Me: I will teach you the fear of the Lord". You must go to Him for teaching. Ask Him, "Teach me Thy way, O Lord".

God Hears Children

GOD is so good that He will hear
Whenever children truly pray;
He always lends a gracious ear,
To what the youngest child can say.

His own most holy Book declares,
He loves all seeking children still,
And that He'll hear their feeble prayers,
Just as a tender father will.

He will not scorn an infant tongue,
That thanks Him for His mercies given;
And when by babes His praise is sung,
Their cheerful songs ascend to heaven.

When little children trust His Word,
And seek Him for their Friend and Guide,
Their little voices will be heard,
And they will never be denied.

Going to Bed

WE need sleep for our bodies and for our minds, yet we often forget this. So God makes the sun set, and draws a curtain over the bright sky, and darkness comes. The cows know what it is for, and they come home from pasture. The hens know what it is for, and they go to roost. The little birds fly to their nests. The shopkeepers draw their blinds, the workers go home. The day is over.

"Come, Robbie," says Mother, "it is time for little folk to go to bed." George and Jane are still at their lessons, but Robbie does not ask to be allowed to wait until George goes to bed.

"Yes, Mother," he replies, and upstairs he runs, knowing that his mother will follow shortly. He likes to look out at the night sky, to see the moon and the twinkling stars. Robbie had the idea that the stars were so many eyes by which God looked down on him, watching over him all night.

Now his mother comes into the room, and Robbie kneels down by her knees and thanks the Lord for His goodness to him through another day. He prays to be made an obedient child, to be helped to speak the truth, and to be kept from getting angry and saying naughty words. And he asks God to forgive him all his sins, for Christ's sake.

It is not just saying our prayers that is important. We must also feel in our hearts what we say. So, when you say your prayers, you must not be thinking of something else. You must think of what you are saying, and feel it in your heart. God not only hears the words that you speak, but also sees how you feel in your heart. Robbie, though he is only a little boy, knows that, and he tries to feel all that he says to God.

When we are in trouble of any kind, or when we are sorry for anything that we have done, or when we are afraid, we must pray to God to forgive us and help us and take care of us. Robbie does, I know. Then he gets into bed, and his mother tucks him in. She gives him a goodnight kiss, and then goes downstairs.

Often Robbie falls asleep repeating a verse of God's Word that he has learned. Here is a verse about going to sleep which you may learn:

> I will both lay me down in peace
> And quiet sleep will take;
> Because Thou only me to dwell
> In safety, Lord, dost make.

(Psalm 4:8)

Mother Puss

OUR cat often has kittens! One day, her two tiny kittens were trying to crawl out of their low box. Puss did not like this. Later, I saw her sitting up in another box in a higher place, with her kittens beside her. It was a much deeper box, and she looked at me as if to say, ''They will be much safer here!''. When I put the box on the ground in a corner outside she did not like this at all. She moved her kittens to a place on top of our dog's box. Perhaps she thought our dog, Simbi, who is her friend, would look after them! How cleverly she protected her kittens.

Another day one of her kittens got lost! I could hear it crying in the space in the roof but no one could find it. All day Mother Puss searched and called, keeping the other kitten right beside her. Then late in the evening I heard loud miaows and went through to see what was wrong. Puss came forward proudly to show me her two kittens! She had finally succeeded where we had completely failed. After that neither kitten was allowed to stray far from Mother Puss.

I'm sure you know that these clever creatures were created by God, and also that He created them for His glory. You also know that God created you. Do you ever think about that? And do you ever think about the special purpose for which God made you? The first answer in the Shorter Catechism tells us why God made us. It says, ''Man's chief end is to glorify God, and to enjoy Him forever''. That means that we are to love God, and that we are to honour and serve Him. Do you do this?

We need a new heart before we can do this. If you do not have a new heart, you cannot glorify God and you will never be willing to do so. Have you asked God yet to give you a new heart? It is only God who can give it, and He tells you, "Ask, and ye shall receive; seek, and ye shall find".

M. Graham

Listen, Children

IF I was speaking to you instead of writing I would say, "Please listen carefully". I'm sure your teacher in school often says, "Listen, children!". But how does she say it? Sometimes she may say it loudly when the class is rather noisy. Sometimes she says it in a mysterious way, as if she were about to tell you something very secret and exciting. Whatever way she says it you know that she means that you must pay attention to what she says.

Now, children, God is saying to you, "Listen to Me". He says in Psalm 34, "Come, ye children, hearken (or listen) unto Me". He says in the Book of

Proverbs, "Now therefore hearken unto me, O ye children". O yes, He is telling you to pay attention to what He is saying.

When your teacher says, "Listen!" she also means that you must do what she tells you to do. She wants you not only to pay attention but also to obey her instructions. So, when God says, "Listen to Me", He also means that you must do what He says. You must be more than attentive to Him; you must also be obedient to Him.

Do you remember that Jesus taught this lesson by telling a parable? He said that it is not enough for us to be hearers of what God says. We must also be doers. The girl or boy who is a hearer only, and not a doer of what God says, is like the man whom Jesus spoke about in the parable. That foolish man built his house on the sand. The storms came and washed away the sand, and the house came crashing down. But if you are a doer as well as a hearer Jesus says that you are like the man who wisely built his house upon a rock. That house stood safe and sound when the fierce storms came. Those of you who are doers, as well as hearers, of what God says will be very safe when He sends the storms of His anger on disobedient people.

Do you know how God speaks to us today? He speaks to us, of course, in His Word, the Bible. Perhaps you have a friend who cannot come to see you and who cannot phone you. How can you hear from that friend? Yes, that's right, by getting a letter. Your friend speaks to you by writing to you, and you might then say to someone, "I've heard from my friend". Is it not wonderful that God has sent us His letter from heaven by sending us the Bible? You can never say, "God has not spoken to me", or, "I have never heard from Him".

And do you know what God is saying to you? He says many things, but one very important thing He says is that you have sinned against Him. Another thing He says is that you need the Saviour, Jesus Christ, to save you from your sins. He tells you that you must be born again and He also says, "Repent and believe the gospel". And does He not tell you that you must live a holy life?

O, my dear young friends, are you listening carefully to what God is saying to you in His letter from heaven? Are you asking God to make you really able to hear and do what He says? May you be like Samuel. When he was a boy, he listened to God. He paid attention to God, but he also obeyed God, and he served Him all his life. Yes, I do hope you will be like Samuel, who was a doer as well as a hearer.

N. M. Ross

Show Me
Thy Ways

SHOW me Thy ways, O Lord;
Thy paths, O teach Thou me:
And do Thou lead me in Thy truth,
Therein my teacher be:

For Thou art God that dost
To me salvation send,
And I upon Thee all the day
Expecting do attend.

Thy tender mercies, Lord,
I pray Thee to remember,
And loving-kindnesses; for they
Have been of old for ever.

My sins and faults of youth
Do Thou, O Lord, forget:
After Thy mercy think on me,
And for Thy goodness great.

Psalm 25:4-7

Rain

AS I sit at the window, a shower of lovely rain is falling! What a strange way to describe rain, some of you may think; but you think like this because you live in a country which may seem to have too much rain.

Here in Zimbabwe we have rain only between October and April. If it does not rain heavily then it becomes unbearably hot, for there are no clouds to shield us from the sun, which in December is directly overhead. Also the crops will not grow and people will starve. You may hear about famine, but can you imagine what it must be like to have no food, and not to know when you will get any?

Many people today try to live without God and think they do not need Him. But who can provide rain? Man may think he can. Sometimes a method called cloud-seeding is used. An aeroplane flies above the clouds and drops chemicals into suitable clouds, causing the clouds to condense and rain to fall from them. However, it is a very limited amount of rain which falls. Also it has been discovered that there may be bad effects later, so that the weather is even drier than before. In any case, the clouds must first be sent by God. Yes, God's rain in His time is best! Only He can send the rain clouds and cause plentiful, refreshing showers to fall.

Why does God sometimes not send rain? One reason is so that we would remember God and think of Him. Lack of rain, and other natural disasters, are some of God's ways of reminding us that it is wicked to forget Him or ignore Him.

When a tornado hit the school last year some pupils said, "God is here!". That was true, but it is a pity we need a special happening to bring this to our minds. God is always "here". How often do you remember this and act as if you believed it? God says, "Remember now thy Creator in the days of thy youth, while the evil days come not . . .".

M. Graham

A Strange School

I WOULD like to tell you about a very strange kind of school; but first I shall ask you some questions. Where do you think the sin that you see in little boys and girls came from? Do you think they were born with it inside their hearts? Do you believe that your own heart is sinful, and that you were sinful even when you were born?

Many people do not think so, even although the Bible says that we were sinful when we were born. They do not believe that when our first parent, Adam, disobeyed God and became a sinner, they also became sinners. You see, Adam had to take our place before God, and therefore when he sinned, we sinned. So all people, because they have come from Adam, are born with sin. In fact sin was in us before we were born. The Psalmist said he ''was shapen in iniquity'' before he was born.

But there are some people who still say, ''No, that's not true. We are really quite good, and are not as bad as some ministers make us out to be''. Of course, you must not believe what they say. Instead you must believe what God tells you in the Bible about your sinfulness.

Here is another question: Is there anything else, besides the Bible, which shows us that we were born with sinful, bad hearts? How can we tell that we were

47

born with sin inside us? I will try to answer and explain by asking you about a very strange kind of school.

Which of you has ever been to a school, or even a kindergarten or nursery school, where the teacher said one day, "Now children, today I am going to give you a lesson on *how to lie*"? Have you ever attended such a class? I can hear you all saying, "O no! We never went to such a school. We never attended a class where lying was taught." And yet, even very little boys and girls are able to tell lies. How is that?

Some of you remember telling lies when you were very, very young. Where did that wickedness come from? I will tell you. It was in you before you saw the light of day. Then, after you were born and you began to grow up, that wickedness inside you came out in the form of lies and other sins. Jesus says that "*out* of the heart of man" come these evil things. So you see, as the Bible says, our hearts were already "deceitful and desperately wicked" when we were born.

I will explain it another way. Perhaps you remember playing in your home with brothers, sisters or friends. Suddenly you broke one of mother's nice ornaments! You remember also that when Dad or Mum came into the room and asked who had broken it, that *you,* as well as everyone else said, "*Not me!*" without giving the question a second thought. You told a lie! Where did you learn to lie? From your teacher at school? No, it came from your own deceitful heart.

Not only lying but all other sins come from the heart. Where did Cain learn to kill, when he killed his brother? To which school did he go, and which teacher taught him to murder? And so I could go on talking about lots of other sins, about breaking the Sabbath, stealing, disobeying your mother and father, being covetous, and using swear-words. They all come out of the heart, which is sinful.

Do you pray to God to forgive your sins and to save you from your deceitful heart? Do you ask Him to change you and to give you a new heart — a heart to believe in Christ, to love the Lord, to delight in what is good and to hate sin? David, when praying for forgiveness, saw that his sin came from within. But at the same time he prayed, ''Create in me a clean heart, O God; and renew a right spirit within me''. Is that not a good prayer for you also to pray?

D. Vermeulen.

The Pitcher Plant

THERE is as beautiful looking plant called the *pitcher plant,* which grows in most tropical parts of the world. A pitcher is a kind of jug, and the ends of the leaves

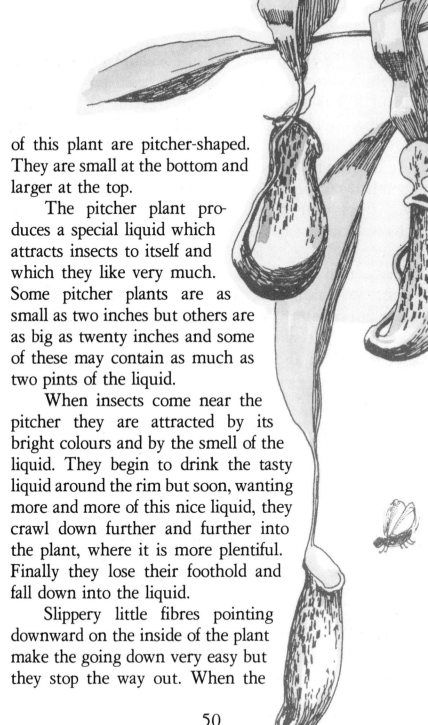

of this plant are pitcher-shaped.
They are small at the bottom and
larger at the top.

The pitcher plant pro-
duces a special liquid which
attracts insects to itself and
which they like very much.
Some pitcher plants are as
small as two inches but others are
as big as twenty inches and some
of these may contain as much as
two pints of the liquid.

When insects come near the
pitcher they are attracted by its
bright colours and by the smell of the
liquid. They begin to drink the tasty
liquid around the rim but soon, wanting
more and more of this nice liquid, they
crawl down further and further into
the plant, where it is more plentiful.
Finally they lose their foothold and
fall down into the liquid.

Slippery little fibres pointing
downward on the inside of the plant
make the going down very easy but
they stop the way out. When the

50

insect tries to climb out of the plant these little spikes are like an army of swords lined up against it. Escape is impossible. The insect struggles but its strength is soon used up, and at last it drowns in the very thing it so much desired.

What a picture this is, young people, of the way of sin and Satan. They would tempt us by what looks so nice and seems so good at the time, but in the end it traps us and destroys us. The little insects are deceived by the plant with its sweet-tasting liquid. They think that the plant has something nice to offer them, but they find out too late that it only takes away all they have — it even takes away their lives.

So it is with sin and Satan. They are deceivers. It is said of Satan, in Revelation 12:9, that he deceives the whole world. The Word of God warns us against the ''deceitfulness of sin'' in Hebrews 3:3. To be deceived means to be fooled. You think that you are going to get something nice, and it seems enjoyable for a while, but then things change and you are instead a prisoner. The deceiving things of sin and Satan may taste sweet for a time but they will soon turn bitter. You will be held as Satan's prisoner and you will be with him in hell.

But we have all sinned and have been caught in Satan's snares, and there is only One who can save us from Satan's prison. That is the Lord Jesus Christ. He died on the cross for sinners and there paid the debt for sin. The wages of sin, which is death, He has endured for His people. So all who receive Him as their Saviour are freed from the judgment of eternal death.

Where are you? Are you running after Satan's sweet-tasting, deceiving sins and held captive by him? Or are you saved, set free by Jesus Christ and serving Him? Be warned by the pitcher plant!

Matthew

JESUS was one day walking along the road near the Sea of Galilee. He noticed a man working beside the road. The man's name was Matthew, but sometimes he was called Levi instead. A lot of traders passed along that road carrying lots of things to sell in other places far away. It was Matthew's job to collect money for the government from those traders.

Matthew was probably very busy at his work when Jesus came along, but he was not to work there any longer. Jesus wanted him to come with Him. So He called to Matthew, ''Follow Me''.

Did Matthew obey Jesus? Yes, he did. And he always went with Jesus wherever Jesus wanted him to go. So when Jesus went to Jerusalem Matthew went too, along with all the other disciples like Peter and James and John. He saw all the wonderful things that Jesus did; he listened to all the wonderful things that Jesus said. And when the time came for Jesus to come back to the Sea of Galilee Matthew came back with Him. He followed Jesus to all sorts of different places.

But when Jesus told Matthew to follow Him He wanted something more from Matthew; He wanted Matthew to obey Him — in everything. He wanted Matthew to do everything that He told Him. We must remember that Jesus is not an ordinary man, because Jesus is God. We must always obey God. How good it was for Matthew that he was willing to follow Jesus!

Do you know that Jesus is saying the same thing to you as He said to Matthew? Yes, He is telling you to follow Him. Not from place to place, like Matthew followed Him. But He wants you to obey Him — always, wherever you go.

Remember that it is Jesus who said, ''Suffer little children to come unto me''. If you come to Him, He will lead you safely through all the difficulties and dangers that everybody has to meet. He is the Good Shepherd who takes care of all His sheep, the little ones as well as the big ones.

Perhaps you are saying to yourself that you do not understand what it means to come to Jesus and to follow Him. You can understand how Matthew could follow Jesus, when Jesus was walking along a road near the Sea of Galilee. But Jesus is now in heaven. So what does it mean for you?

Should you not tell Jesus all about it? Pray to Him. Ask Him to make you understand what it means to follow Him, and what it means to come to Him. Ask Him to make you really able to obey Him. And ask Him to make you really want to obey Him.

K. D. Macleod

What Sydney Owed

IF you owe money to somebody it means that you have to pay the money to him. I read in an old book about a ten-year-old boy who thought that his mother owed him money. His name was Sydney and he was sure that his mother should pay him for helping her, just as a boss gives wages to those who work for him.

However, Sydney was not bold enough to ask his mother for the money. What was he to do? Suddenly he had a bright idea — or so he thought. He would write a list or bill of what his mother owed him and leave it in a place in the house where she would find it.

Sydney worked out what he thought his mother owed him and wrote it all down on the bill. In those days a penny was written like this: *1d.* Twelve pennies made up one shilling, which was written like this: *1s.*

Next morning Sydney's mother was very surprised indeed to see the bill lying on her kitchen table. This is what Sydney wrote:

Mother Owes Sydney	
For getting coal six times	6d
For fetching wood lots of times	6d
For going errands twice	4d
For being a good boy	2d
Total	1s 6d

His mother read the bill but said nothing. That evening Sydney found the bill, with 1s 6d as payment, on his plate at tea time. Underneath it was another bill. He picked it up and read it. This is what he read:

Sydney Owes Mother	
For his happy home for ten years	*Nothing*
For his food and clothes	*Nothing*
For helping him do his lessons	*Nothing*
For nursing him through illness	*Nothing*
Total	*Nothing*

Sydney had hardly finished it when the tears began to come to his eyes. He felt so ashamed when he saw how kind his mother was and how mean and selfish he was. He knew that if she asked him for money for doing all these things for him that he could never pay her. He took the 1s 6d out of his pocket, rushed to his mother, flung his arms round her neck, and exclaimed, "O mother, I was so mean; please forgive me! Here is the money; I don't want it. And I will do lots and lots of things to help you."

Dear children, you can never pay your mother or father for all their kindness to you, but that does not mean that you owe them nothing. You owe them honour, for God says, "Honour thy father and thy mother". To honour them means to respect them, love them and obey them. So you owe them love, don't you? God tells us, "Love one another". The best way to show your love to your parents is to obey them. So you owe them obedience. God tells you, "Children, obey your parents in the Lord, for this is right".

N. M. Ross

A Perfect Friend

THERE's a Friend for little children
Above the bright blue sky,
A Friend who never changes,
Whose love will never die;
Our earthly friends may fail us,
And change with changing years,
This Friend is always worthy
Of that dear Name He bears.

There's a rest for little children
Above the bright blue sky,
Who love the blessed Saviour,
And to the Father cry;
A rest from every trouble,
From sin and sorrow free,
Where every little pilgrim
Shall rest eternally.

There's a home for little children
Above the bright blue sky,
Where Jesus reigns in glory,
A home of peace and joy.
No home on earth is like it,
Nor can with it compare:
For every one is happy,
Nor can be happier there.

Did You Ever
See a Soul?

A GODLY minister met a doctor who did not believe the Bible and who despised Christianity.

"So you preach to save souls," the doctor said.

"Yes, I do," the minister replied; for he believed that the Word of God which he preached is able to save souls.

"Did you ever see a soul?" asked the doctor.

"No," replied the minister.

"Did you ever hear a soul?" "No."

"Did you ever taste a soul?" "No."

"Did you ever smell a soul?" "No."

"Did you ever feel a soul?" the doctor finally asked.

"Yes, in a way I have," said the minister. "God made me feel that I have a soul and that it had to be saved."

The doctor then said to the minister, "At least four of your five senses say there is no soul. That's four against one." In this way the doctor tried to show that there is no such thing as a soul.

The minister turned to the doctor and asked him, "Tell me, doctor, did you ever see a pain?"

"No," replied the doctor.

"Did you ever hear a pain?" "No."

"Did you ever taste a pain?" "No."

"Did you ever smell a pain?" "No."

"Did you ever feel a pain?"

Of course the doctor had to reply, "Yes."

"Well then," said the preacher, "Four of your five senses seem to show that there is no pain".

Both the minister and the doctor knew that it would be silly and untrue to say that there is no such thing as pain; but I don't know if the doctor ever thought that it is just as untrue to say that we do not have a soul.

Do not believe those who say that you do not have a soul. Believe God when He is telling you that your soul must be saved. How awful it is for anyone to lose his soul in hell.

Remember what Jesus says: "What shall it profit a man, if he shall gain the whole world, and lose his own soul? Or what shall a man give in exchange for his soul?"

May God bring you by His Holy Spirit to believe in Jesus Christ, so that your soul may be saved.

The Blind Boy

I READ in an old book about a blind boy in a mission school in Syria. Like some other boys in this school he had learned to read the Bible, but it was a special Bible

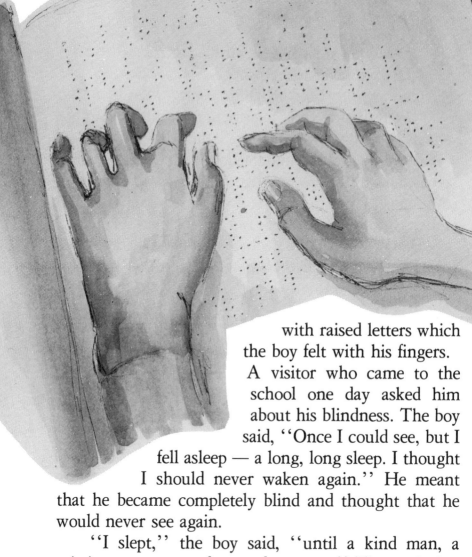

with raised letters which the boy felt with his fingers.

A visitor who came to the school one day asked him about his blindness. The boy said, "Once I could see, but I fell asleep — a long, long sleep. I thought I should never waken again." He meant that he became completely blind and thought that he would never see again.

"I slept," the boy said, "until a kind man, a missionary, came and opened my eyes." Then pointing to his blind eyes he said, "Not these eyes". Lifting up his fingers he said, "He opened these eyes". The boy meant that the missionary taught him to read with his fingers. "Now these eyes see the sweet words of Jesus," the boy added.

So much did the boy love "the sweet words of Jesus" that he wanted others to know them, and he often carried a cripple boy on his back to the school so that he too would read and hear the gospel.

Can you imagine the two boys going to school? The cripple boy would be eyes for the blind boy, and the blind boy would be legs for the cripple boy. I do not think that you would ever forget the sight. What would be your thoughts?

You ought to think that there is no better use for your eyes than to read the Word of God, that there is no better use for your legs than to take you to the house of God, and that there is no better use for both than to help others to come to hear God's Word. I hope you will think about that.

Now, if you turn to John, chapter 9, you will read about a man who was born blind and who was made to see by Jesus. Jesus still does a very wonderful thing when He opens the eyes of the understanding of a sinner, and then leads that person to heaven.

There was once a blind Christian who had been born blind. Although the eyes of his understanding had been opened to see Jesus, he looked forward to the time when he would see Jesus with the eyes of his body. He said, "I have never seen anyone, so Jesus will be the first person I will ever see, for my eyes will be opened in heaven".

Abridged from the story by the late Rev. John Tallach.

From Dirty Rags
to Perfect Paper

THE paper in this page was made from wood pulp, but some kinds of special paper are made from rags. Long ago, all paper was made from rags. Each paper mill had a large room in which rags were stored until they were needed for making more paper.

Queen Victoria once visited a paper mill. The owner of the mill showed her through the mill, including the ''rag room''. When she saw the differently coloured and soiled rags she wondered how they could be made into white paper. ''How can these rags *ever* be made white?'' she asked.

The owner of the mill replied, ''We use a chemical process, Madam, by which we can take the colour out of even the red and scarlet rags''.

Some time later, the Queen received a gift of some of the most beautiful white paper she had ever seen. It looked most expensive — like very, very good writing paper. On each sheet were the letters of her own name, and probably her coat of arms as well. Along with this gift there was a letter. The Queen saw that it was from the mill owner whose paper mill she had visited. This is part of what he wrote:

''Will Her Majesty be pleased to accept a specimen of my paper, with the assurance that every sheet was manufactured out of the dirty rags which she saw? I trust that the result is such that Her Majesty may admire it.

"Will Her Majesty also allow me to say that I have had a good many sermons preached to me by what I see in my mill? I can understand how the Lord Jesus Christ can take the poor heathen, and the vilest of the vile, and make them clean; and how, though their sins be as scarlet, He can make them white as snow.

"And I can see how He can put His own name upon them. And just as those rags, now transformed, may go into the palace and be admired; so poor sinners can be cleansed, and be received into the palace by the Great King."

This is the cleansing and the change which we all need because our sins have made us filthy, and have deeply stained us like red and scarlet dye. Only God can change you, and He is graciously calling you to come to Him so that He may make you clean.

Seek with your whole heart that He would make you willing and able to obey His call: "Come now, and let us reason together, saith the Lord: though your sins be as scarlet, they shall be as white as snow; though they be red like crimson, they shall be as wool" (Isaiah 1:18).

Serving God
with Gladness

ALL people that on earth do dwell,
Sing to the Lord with cheerful voice.
Him serve with mirth, His praise forth tell,
Come ye before Him and rejoice.

Know that the Lord is God indeed;
Without our aid He did us make:
We are His flock, He doth us feed,
And for His sheep He doth us take.

O enter then His gates with praise,
Approach with joy His courts unto:
Praise, laud, and bless His name always,
For it is seemly so to do.

For why? The Lord our God is good,
His mercy is for ever sure;
His truth at all times firmly stood,
And shall from age to age endure.

Psalm 100